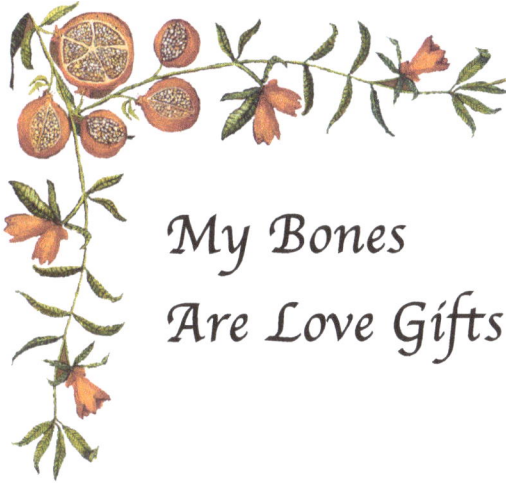

My Bones
Are Love Gifts

My Bones Are Love Gifts

poems and interior art by
Dawn Sperber

SHANTI ARTS PUBLISHING
BRUNSWICK, MAINE

My Bones Are Love Gifts

Published by Shanti Arts Publishing
Cover art by Irene Hardwicke Olivieri
Creative design by Dawn Sperber
Cover design and layout by Coverkitchen
Interior design by Shanti Arts Designs

Shanti Arts LLC
193 Hillside Road
Brunswick, Maine 04011
shantiarts.com

Printed in the United States of America

ISBN: 978-1-956056-63-1 (softcover)

Library of Congress Control Number: 2022948534

*Dedicated to that shift in the wind
that brings in the magic.*

Contents

Acknowledgments 9

Fool Card 12
My Bones Are Love Gifts 14
You Used to Be the World 17
The Beautiful Mess of Melting 19
We Take All the Luck We Can Get 23
These Days of Leaf Shadows 24
The Turning Time 27
Gears of the Night 31
Blue Dawn 33
Ghost of Surprise Drafts 36
Heartbeat Behind the Glass 38
Like Sand (Or Sugar) 43
My Cloak Slips Off 44
See What the Rain Brings 46
Cycle of Precipitation 48
A Wild Thing Full of Magnets 50
Thirst in the Day 53
Two Views 54
Shaky Lines 57
Wake Up! 58
Welcome 60
Shadow-dog 62
Spiders Bite Me in My Sleep 65
Light in the Night of My Body 67
The Woman Who Is This Day 71
Petal Booklet 74
Gentle, Gentle, Go My Friend 76
A Small Love, Obviously Wild 78
Come to Me, Goodness 81
What Are We Waiting For? 82

Acknowledgments

The author extends much gratitude to the editors of the following publications in which these poems first appeared:

Going Down Swinging: "Spiders Bite Me in My Sleep" (2020); "Fool Card" (2011)

NANO Fiction: "We Take All the Luck That We Can Get" (2016)

ONE ART: A Journal of Poetry: "Gears of the Night" (2020)

Third Wednesday: "Ghost of Surprise Drafts" (2010)

We'Moon: "A Wild Thing Full of Magnets" (2020); "My Bones Are Love Gifts" (2017); "My Cloak Slips Off" (2018); "What Are We Waiting For?" (2015)

❖

Bright gratitude to Irene Harwicke Olivieri for sharing her amazing artwork *The Painter and her skeleton* (2019), which blesses this book's cover. Olivieri lives in Santa Fe, New Mexico, painting in the mysterious workshop of nature. She raises caterpillars, spiders, succulents, and cacti, and enjoys exploring the wilderness and helping wildlife. Learn more about her paintings and the evocative ideas behind them at irenehardwickeolivieri.com.

❖

I'm thankful to those who came before me, whose lives helped pave the way for me to share my voice as a woman writer. Thank you to the loved ones I carry inside me, in my blood and my memories. Thanks to my mom, Becky Sperber, for taking me to the library on the weekends when I was little and for encouraging intuition and storytelling. Thanks to my dad,

Matthew Sperber, for raising me to revere books. Heartfelt appreciation to my soul bro Mattie Greenman, who listened to my poems' recordings on early mornings with his coffee for years, just because he loved them. What a gift to be heard. I hope his spirit fingers have no trouble turning these pages. I'm grateful to many allies for their support, including my brother Sean Sperber; Dan Mueller; Diane Walker; my aunts, Pat Demarest and Kathleen Ewing; Melanie Unruh, Sam Tetangco Ocena, Jenn Simpson, and the Plume: A Writer's Companion community; A Room Of Her Own Foundation; the University of New Mexico MFA program; and the inspiring friends who've shared their magic during the journey. Deep appreciation to Christine Cote and Shanti Arts Publishing for their excellent work on this book, and to Xavier Comas and Coverkitchen for help with the cover design.

And thank you, Spirit, for your beautiful love and presence.

(deep curtsy)

Fool Card

We're always beginning something
and ending other things.
Some noticed and big events,
and some as casual as finally dropping the napkin
you forgot you were holding in your hand.
Or throwing away the receipts
and old tickets you'd carried in your bag.
Or smiling goodbye to a friend,
and they may not know it,
but you mean it permanent, Goodbye.

Ending some things. And beginning others.
All the time. I guess that's what time is, in a way.
The story-fabric of starts and stops.

And since this is the way of things,
of tiny and large cycles both, everything overlapping,
a storyteller knows each moment
holds the introduction of one tale or another,
and in that same moment,
and also the ones previous and following,
are stories concluding.

The story-fabric will reveal what is to come
and in what light to view this beginning.
I am mortal and trying, breathing in, out.
I am a character in the story,
and my living leaves words
like footsteps on the pages behind me.
Up ahead the book is blank,
pages opaque as the surface of stones.

Sometimes, it seems so brave,
the steps we mortals make.
Dancing on the cliff edge
with the rocks trickling down,
we are the tarot's Fool card,
blind to what is to come.
And yet we continue, give it a go,
and as we walk into story developments
and they happen to us, around us,
that's the way we find out.

Anything could happen, and we go forward,
live it anyway.
We have no choice.

Peace

My Bones Are Love Gifts

I breathe in my ancestors and their enemies.
I breathe in dinosaurs, and sneeze.
I inhale mountain ranges, and sigh.
I breathe in lovers and betrayers,
and the houses they all lived in,
the blankets that covered
their sleeping vulnerability,
the baby teeth they lost
and buried under the porch.
Inhale, exhale.
We are each other.

My body is a composite, like variegated sand,
made of the past and medium for future forms.
Star particles look out at the horizon through my eyes,
and death is reborn through my newly dividing cells.
We own so little, really,
just share and receive the meal of our lives
in existence's communal kitchen,
full of delicacies and compost,
just like our bodies,
and our lifetime's storylines.

My teeth are made of ancient dynasties.
My yoni is concocted
from the water molecules of a river,
once rushing, that carved the canyons.
My brain contains particles
from mythical beasts we retain no record of
and smells like lightning from the storms
that excite and race across my synapses.

—continued

Ostara

Some of my memories
are recorded in someone else's voice
and refer to a previous face in the mirror.
My bones are love gifts
from elders millennia past.
Inside my veins travels gold dust
that sifted down the mountainside,
back when their peaks were so much taller,
when we were all so different, and yet even then,
we were one and the same.

I raise my drink and sip particles
of the footed fish who made its way
through the discomfort of evolution—
and after swallowing, momentarily,
I ache with desire to grow into an environment
that should seemingly kill me.
Such is the first taste
of all magnificent inclinations.

I breathe in the dust of who came before,
who never knew me, and yet we're one.

You Used to Be the World

You used to be the world. Do you remember?
You had fire inside, liquid fire, honest and burning.
That was your heart, and your heart filled you up.
You encased your heart in stone.
That was to give you shape, make you durable.
And then your skin; we all loved your skin,
pliant soil, all manner of plants, trees, wildflowers.
You were covered in food, and homes.
All the creatures lived on, and of you.
And your water; my god, we'd never seen
love in a tangible form before,
and didn't we drink you up.
My sweet world,
solar system child,
grandchild of the cosmos.
Do you remember how it was?
You had no head;
you knew we were all one, connected,
and you, me, all of us were the same thing.
Remember back before we had faces,
when we spun through space, growing?
When I was you, and so were the elephants?
Our hearts were fire, and our love was water,
and that was before those were opposites.
I can't explain how different.
Shut your eyes; that may help.

—continued

Before we developed
and believed in divisions,
we had space pressed
against our shared skin.
You remember, don't you?
It smelled calm like falling asleep,
and felt
like
shift
ing
vel
vet.

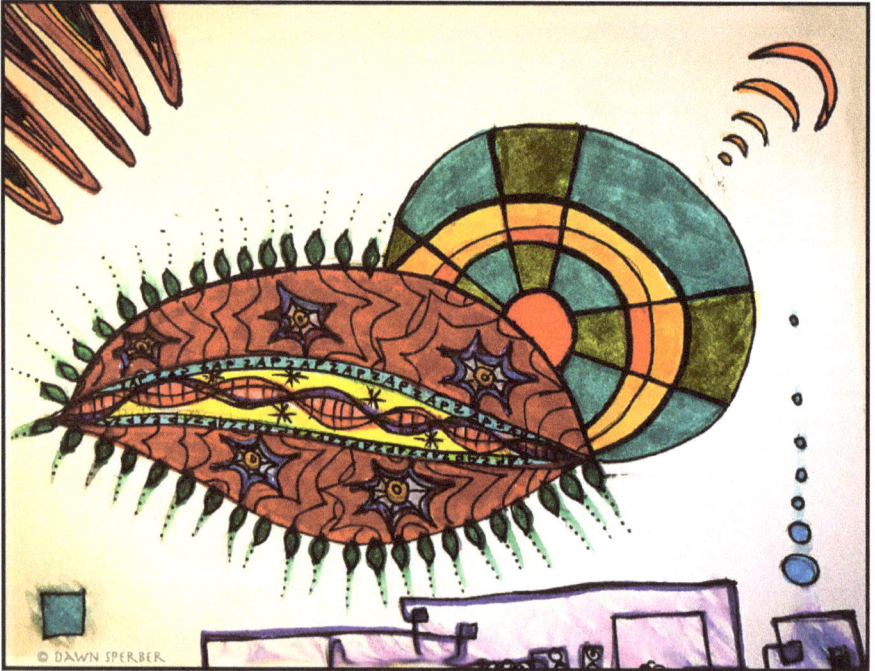

Chemical Processes & Enlightenment

The Beautiful Mess of Melting

I used to be an ice sculpture of a woman,
and I posed in a dark cave.
No one saw me but spiders, and the white and gray
dots that float in darkness.
My thoughts had crystalline structures,
like math problems that all added up,
except for the three sharp fractures
originating around my heart
and rivering through my frozen terrain.

I was icy-clean, self-referential,
and I made perfect sense,
there alone in my dark cold cave,
in my smooth, stiff posture.
Biggest problem was I couldn't dance that way.

It was those three rivering fractures
that woke me.
The ticking of their inching cracks
echoed against my cave walls,
getting louder like an alarm clock about to ring.
I didn't mind being frozen, until
the cracks threatened to divide me,
and then all I wished was to gather
up and twirl like a whirlpool.

My melting was sudden,
and then I spun out of my cave's mouth
like a woman-sized hurricane.
I've been dancing the spiral dance ever since.
I leave streaks, drips, and puddles behind me,
which I call drinks of water, and some call a mess.
I've had people shake their dripping sponges at me,

—continued

Queen o' the Sea

and one family member twisted her ankle
when she slipped on one of my puddles.
She still holds onto her grudge
like it's a fat white cat,
and feeds it morsels off her plate.

Yet I carry on.
There's always a song in my head
and a good beat to dance to.
What am I going to do,
politely gather my waters like rocks
and keep them clutched to my chest?
Those hard days are far away
as a dream I already woke from.
Now, I'd only spill right through my fingers.

I'm less proper these days, muddier.
And also a better dancer.
I'm always damp, with moss growing
on my dresses, algae in my elbows,
and wildflowers blooming along my cheeks.
And when I laugh hard, my chest still leaks.
Then, hummingbirds swoop by
to drink from between my breasts.
I never feel the sharp of their beaks,
but shut my eyes and sway
to their thrumming wings,
like a sweetheart's serenade.

Prayer

We Take All the Luck We Can Get

In New Mexico, we take all the luck we can get.
When it streams along the red dirt road like rainwater,
we bend down and scoop it up in our empty to-go cups.
Then, we duck behind a piñon and pour it over our heads,
open our mouths and drink some too, just like a hobo shower.
We love the luck and what it does to our waking dreams.
How it makes us shine.
There are magnets in the water that call our intentions
from over the mountains to our hands like trained birds.
Everyone, from adobe wall-builder to hermit oil painter,
everyone out here trying, loves to hear them sing
and stops to listen when at last they sing again.
Sometimes the luck showers us from the blue sky
like warm summer rain, every now and then.
We stay attentive, ready for it.

These Days of Leaf Shadows

Yesterday, I kept seeing bird shadows
fly past the curtains.
But then they were so many birds, I got curious
and realized their flights paired
with the swamp cooler's growling,
and that was because they were actually
leaves blowing in the wind gusts.
It was the particular loveliness
that is a sunny November day
casting gold light through the curtains
and streaming leaf silhouettes across the windows.

There are leaves all over right now,
racing and gossiping, collecting in circles,
the leaves of various trees all congregating,
and then rushing in a great hurry
from one side of the courtyard to the other,
or trading sides of the street,
sometimes synchronized as circus performers,
sometimes aimless as partiers on a four-day drunk.
It's a different world when the leaves
are released from the trees and intermingling.

They love that they are so untethered;
they can't help but respond to each passing wind.
And I can relate to that.
Sometimes there's nothing like
responding without trying to,
seeing the evidence of how you're affected.
The leaves whisk and crackle with surprise and fun,
to see how the wind tussles, flies them high,
low, straight to the sky, and sometimes
grinds them to bits against the wall.

—continued

Leave It

Everything that happens is done to them.
They spent all last season focused on growing,
budding and stretching, then oxygenating
and doing chlorophyll processes.
Now, their work is over,
and look how they're dawdled about
as if they never had a stem or rooted tree.

Once the leaves drop, they enter the mix
and mingle of the bluster world.
The world is a party, and wind is love.
It makes them fly and sometimes crushes them.
The surprise is what they most adore,
how they have no idea what's coming,
and no weight to resist the wind's fickle push.

The season is named for one part of their journey:
fall. But there's more, because then follows
the abandon of rushing, blown about, flying.
In autumn, a leaf has no desire
for preservation, no need to last.
It's the ultimate condition for adventure.

In a few weeks, most of these leaves will be gone.
But now they're still bright yellow,
bright green, popping red, orange—
and soft, trailing their still fresh fingers
across the ground, spiraling up.
They're everywhere,
as if they always will be.

The Turning Time

It's definitely the turning time.
The air is grayish brown.
Grocery bags run across the street,
then raise to the air in manic possession,
jerking high and low.
A red flier whisks by and shoots
high up into a red rolling dot.

Two girls on bikes turn my corner,
and are soon yelling
as they pedal slowly,
hair gone active and insane.
A man walks around my corner,
and the bald top of his head stays still,
but the shoulder-length blond hair
encircling it lifts straight up,
then shoots out like wings,
as his mouth scowls and screws up
on one side of his face.
He deliberately stomps on.

What I can often forget about spring
is the turning wind that brings it in.
This black dog reclines
in the shadow of the trashcan.
He holds still and shuts his eyes
as his fur raises and falls,
and his tail shivers,
its soft tip blown back and forth.
He's so gentle as he withstands the gusts
that I watch as if he's teaching a lesson,
like how when an especially strong gust comes in,
he slowly lowers his head to his paws
stretched neatly before him.

—continued

I can imagine this dog in any country,
in the city or mountains,
anywhere in the world where there's wind,
which is everywhere.
(Now, the heavy door animates to open
and slam shut,
which I translate as "Damn right,"
though I don't usually speak Door.)
Now, the dog's gone, and all the trashcan has
is its squashed, wobbling silhouette.
I think we all miss the patient dog.

Nothing can sit still in this spring wind.
Everything gets touched,
jostled, shivered around,
and everything unattached takes to the wind.
Each year's the same.
Spring wind strips away the dead leaves,
readies the branches, and blows
till the seeds and pollen fly.
In order to grow,
first, you must be blustered.

© DAWN SPERBER

Float

Telescope

Gears of the Night

for Jennifer Simpson

The night before Christmas,
people were busy in their lit houses.
The moon kept revolving all the same.
The tide headed out, then returned,
headed out, and returned.
The shoreline breathed the rhythm.
The bugs bored into the trunks
of the trees behind the factory.
Tick, tick, tick went their tiny teeth.
The metal slats across the overpass
clattered each time a car drove past:
clac-clack, clac-clack.
Then, the traffic cleared
and only crickets sang.
Out from the darkness, a pickup sped by
—*clac-clack*—
and the pigeons under the bridge
lifted in a swirl and swooped away.
There was a snail working
his way up a drainpipe.
He'd stopped and rested some hours,
his slime hardening on the corrugated metal.
With no fanfare at all,
he returned to his journey up the pipe.
The moon noticed but said nothing.
Why would it.
On the eve of Christmas,
outside of the busy, lit boxes,
the gears of the night turned onward.

NM Wishes

Blue Dawn

Blue dawn finds me again in transition
between out of town and entry into the next town.
The train slides through the dark, dim fields on either side,
and the sky performs poetry of sublime new light
over the northern lip of the silhouette mountains.

The slate fields fog up;
a pink streak arrives low in the gray sky.
The cars *chunk-a-chunk* on the tracks below,
hurtling along at 80 miles an hour.
Cows appear in fields, and I levitate by.

It was pitch black when I biked to the station.
The sky went dark violet while I waited
on the Albuquerque train platform
for my Rio Rancho temp job's route.
Now, the sky is dark speckled gray.

I yawn, and a shaft of gold light breaks
over the mountains, cuts through the dim hue,
and illuminates the gilded curls
of steam rising
from a field's grazing cows.

For a moment, the beauty is so sudden,
my throat gets hard and tight,
but the train speeds on,
and the next moment brings
a struggling reservation town.

—continued

The small houses are patched with colorful scrap-boards,
among the herds of gutted, dead cars.
Some ribby dogs lope by, heads low.
On the last shack of the little village
—a gray teddy bear in a roof gutter, unfound.

Then, rolling sagebrush land claims the view,
with sunlit tawny foothills nearby,
and beyond them, blue silhouette mountains
echo further and further
back in the distance, so it seems

they continue forever,
and there are no cities in that direction,
nothing but desert and mountains,
sand and clay, sage,
rabbits, lizards, coyotes.

Each morning, I wish the train would keep going
and I wouldn't get off at this growing town of strip malls,
my helmet banging against my arm,
my bike tires bouncing off the train step,
followed by my footfalls.

Now, my train ride is over, and I sit in the shuttle bus
headed toward my job's industrial building,
watching the sky pull off her veils like Salome.
First went the black one; then the violet, the gray,
then the mother-bedroom-blue,

and now, we've reached the part of the dance
where she's showing her range of pastel scarves.
I like this part very much. It's brief but not yet over.
Soon will come the brilliantine sunrays
to dazzle the sky like a beautiful

girl's blond hair, obvious, demanding
attention, changing the scene forevermore.
But not yet. It's still the intimate time right before,

which teaches me that some veils are useful,
to dole out the wonders one by one by one.

I would never know
how windy it is
if that flag weren't screaming
it's streaming.
Blown straight back and rippling.

Right after I see that patriotic rippler,
the shuttle bus pulls up to work and we all get off,
file down the stairs and up the asphalt parking lot,
to wait by the door, for 7:20
when the automatic unlock happens.

I kind of like it in a weird way
nobody else standing here
freezing on the sidewalk
would probably understand.
The men and women's pant legs snap,

pressed flat back, revealing their thin legs,
much more vulnerable than their loose-hanging fit.
We all huddle behind the half-wall's windbreak
like a group of mice or prairie dogs,
less individual and more of a warm-blooded collective,

and it's comforting.
Especially since it's almost 7:20, when the lock switches,
and we file in with our magnetic code badges
to sit like computer chips before our monitors,
for hours and hours of electrical brain work.

I like this proof of our life and heat
and our vulnerable thin legs,
and how we group together like any other animals,
with no other thought than buffering
the early morning spring wind.

Ghost of Surprise Drafts

Snow falls—but no, it doesn't fall—
drifts and flies and fights itself with a bounce,
and hurries backward and leaps up
and races ahead to see what the others are looking at
—o nothing—and tumbles backward again.
This mid-air snow that goes like a song, slow, slow,
then speeding, tumbling, flying backward
like repetition building, crisscrossing,
stippling the air into a spinning lace veil,
so thick and white and fast, and then,
like a song that's wonderful yet ends anyway,
the drift slows, pales, gets thinner,
and fades into the empty air of clarity.

But when it was so fast and racing,
I stepped off the ledge of the moment
into a snowy expanse somewhere,
me, colored dot in the stippled white, arms wide,
fingertips touched, and nose, and eyelids,
and I had on a wide gown of thick green velvet,
a gown trees would love,
and my legs were warmed
by the buoyant red heart
they stood in under my skirt,
that filled out its fat bell shape.

I think a ghost just came inside.
I watched the heavy glass door pull open,
the width of a body, pause, and shut again.
The snow was in a racing moment too,
so it may have been a snow faerie,
my size, who opened the door,
wove through the cluttered room
on snowflaked feet,
and is perhaps sitting across from me even now!

Hello, snow faerie, ghost of surprise drafts.
If you lean under the table,
can you hear my gown's heartbeat?

I imagine when she blushes,
her cheeks tint like
snow beside an apple.

Snow Queen

Heartbeat Behind the Glass

Our blood is racing.
My bedside window wears a beard of frost,
and I say no wonder my head gets cold,
with such a lover breathing down my neck.

My blood steams up windows with my life.
The snow on the ground muffles sounds,
but still-primal, attentive animals can probably stand
by the adobe house and hear my heart beating within,

hear my unconscious breathing song,
in out in out in in outttt in out in out.
The wild ones have such ears, I have no doubt.
Even a domesticated cat like me

can hear a beetle crawling down the tile stairs
in the front room, and that's after most of my life
spent wearing civilization earmuffs.
Most people barely hear a thing,

see only computer screens and streetlights,
while all manner of birds fly by overhead,
who may as well be transparent.
The wild ones, though, are wild.

—continued

The Strength of Roots Underground

They keep their senses sharp as honed knives
in order to eat and stay alive.
The effort leaves them super-powered,
compared to us, who grow duller and softer,

malleable pale bodies sprouting
electronic wires and hard-drive minds.
Who's really stronger?
Depends on the environment to answer that one.

Each night at the house, I hear the coyotes
howl and call throughout the land.
Individuals begin a song, and then others answer,
pick up the mania, till everyone's screaming,

finding each other out and forming a pack.
Sometimes, they get so close and loud.
Last night, I kissed my lover in the driveway
as the pink dusk fled and night took over,

while precisely arranged stars looked down
to find constellations in our manes' spiral designs.
We kissed a long time, and when he finally
drove away, he had to swerve hard

around a large coyote by the mailbox,
almost as tall as a wolf, just standing there.
What drew him, I wonder?
Maybe it was our irregular heartbeats,

our quick breaths and heat.
Excitements can be indistinguishable
from a distance, and one manner
of feast can seem like another.

My lover drove away and I returned inside,
and the coyote, what did he do?
Maybe prowled by my window
snuffling at the pheromones in my sweat.

The barrier between outside and inside
is like the division between wild and tame.
I roll over in bed, look at the crystalline window,
and wipe a finger through the ice.

I understand the barriers aren't so impenetrable.
That's why I can smell
the wind through the door
and sweet grasses thawing in the sunshine.

Purpling

Like Sand (Or Sugar)

I keep remembering the last night my dad was alive,
when I reached into my backpack's pocket
to grab a candle to light for him,
but the candle crumbled and squeezed
through my fingers like sand, or—
"Sugar," Mattie sings, walking in the door now,
crooning the word I was considering
editing out of my sentence.
"Dundun Dundun Dundun, oh, honey honey."
That was the night I didn't light a candle
because it got crushed on the trip
and poured through my fingers
like fine brown sugar,
as if the wax were something sweet.

My Cloak Slips Off

Maybe in the dark, my form disappears.
I may be essence, like a scent
wearing a cloak of a body,
but sometimes, when I'm not asked a question
and don't have to respond, there in the dark
when I am unaware, my cloak slips off.
And rather than having a body that sits
or stands or lies down,
I hover, waft, undulate, and small stars shoot
through the cloud of scent that is my true being.
Maybe mirrors lie, I look completely different,
and I have never really seen myself.
It could be my eyes that prevent the seeing,
by defining a form to witness,
instead of admitting
the mystery that is a self.

© DAWN SPERBER

Lotus Light

See What the Rain Brings

Sometimes, I feel sensations from invisible sources
and wonder if they're from an adjacent lifetime
I'm living somewhere else.
Now, as I sit in the dim living room
with the roof gutters dripping from this recent May rain,
I can also somehow feel a hand cupping the back of my head,
fingers twining through my silky clean hair,
the feel of my neck arching back till my skin gets tight.

I'm here alone in a straight-backed chair,
but also, I can feel me somewhere where my gravity is shifting
and I'm leaned back, held from dropping, and then kissed.
It's a solid and full kiss, just perfect, going on somewhere
so that I can feel it too, just a bit, as if,
like a jellyfish, parts of me reach out in all directions,
out to where I can't see, but a part of me is there anyway.

Maybe that other life is from a choice I didn't make,
or is from the future, or is someone else's
memory of me from the past.
I become aware of the sensations happening anyway,
whether I understand them or not.
And along with them is a dark peripheral vision,
where everything is navy blue with pale streaks.
That's all I know, and that I like it.
And then life continues on.

I mean, if I don't trim down experience
to agree with what people are already talking about, this—
this is what my life is like. With these extra moments
no one mentions, or they try to label out of validity.
But really, life contains a lot more
than what most people agree on.

© DAWN SPERBER

Turned Around

Cycle of Precipitation

I miss you like a rip in my water body,
trickling out my essentials.
And when I say you,
I mean the you who changes
to look like all I long for,
my had's, and my not-yet-but-coming's,
and also my never-to-be's.
I'm not pretending to make
a certain kind of sense
or be the winning case in an argument.

I'm simply admitting the rip,
and mourning my drops that leave,
though I know my water body
is made to be full
and will soon be filled again.
It's full moon.
Have I mentioned that yet;
am I more understandable?
In any case, I'm me.
Gotta have one thing reliable.
As reliable as possible, considering…

I am like the ocean.
If you blur your eyes and look again,
I'm a body shape filled with waves,
with foam, sculpted crests,
and the hollows beneath them.
Even my eyes change texture.
I look different by the second.
And amazements and mystery
hide in my depths.

My tide's high today.
My waves are crashing
and reaching for the moon:
within the shapes of my legs

crossed at the knee,
within my raised arm,
and my palm brushing back
my poured ink hair.

My evaporating leak is steaming up
the cups and windows.
Dusted with mist,
my houseplants reach and unfurl.

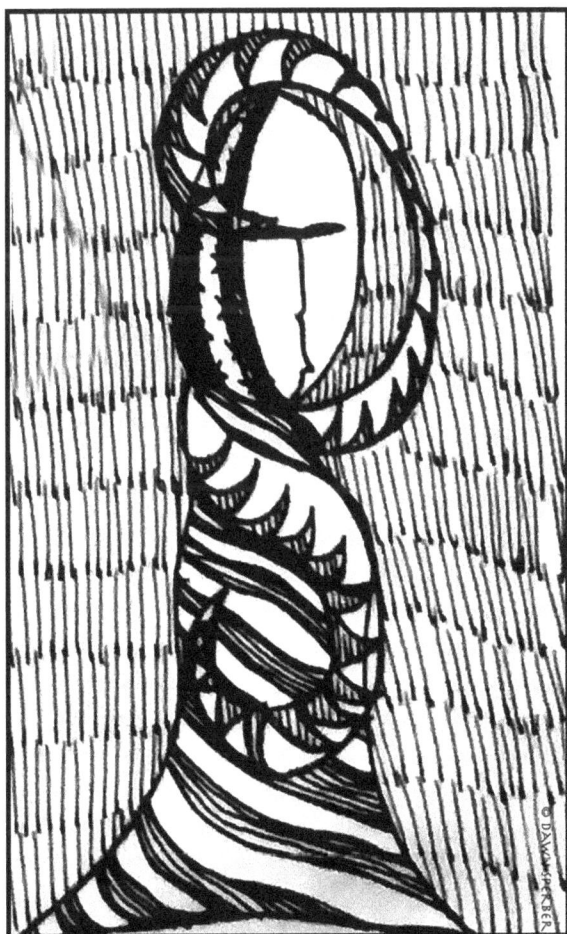

Slick

A Wild Thing Full of Magnets

I've been a mind and ability;
I've been plans and focus
and fiery hopeful belief.
But when you speak,
keys fall through your voice
and go unlocking me,
freeing a body that erupts
beneath my eyes and lips.
My long-lost body,
beautiful and imperfect,
silken-haired and scarred—
a wild thing full of magnets,
now pulled toward you
and all the keys falling
through your voice.

It's magic, to grow legs and feet
and breasts and hands,
and yet, my body confuses time
and disrupts my eagle-eye and dream strategies,
by leaning forward, by wanting and ringing,
ringing like that tinkling pile of keys
left on the floor after
your oblivious magic tricks.
And I say nothing,
go back to my long-term goals,
but I don't fit on the chair anymore.
My legs kick,
my ass bumps the cushion off,
and I'm a wild animal in the house.

—continued

Rainman

My missing half of me returned,
now, I don't fit.
Shoved from my logic dreams,
in a body, I'm lonely.
Yet how can I not be grateful for the trick
and replay how all you did was talk,
and here I unlocked and went unfurling
like I've been a jack-in-the-box all along.

So, now I'm a tangle of hips and arms and belly,
wrapped 'round with one-eyed plans,
but for those minutes when you told a story,
I remembered how to be complete.
Thanks for the unlocking and zap
and the beautiful electricity powering you,
even if now all my hands
get in their own way.
Still, the trick was glorious,
and terrible
and more real than I'd remembered.

Bless your voice's keys.
Now, here I go into this weird, blazing day.

Thirst in the Day

The undone acts still balance full cups of potential,
and we hold them carefully before us
with an elbow angled against spilling
as we run down sidewalks, keeping up with errands,
rushing through a door to snake across the foyer in line,
filling out paperwork and making calls,
jotting down details, getting on and off of buses.

And when there's any spare moment,
bending down a face to the cup of potential
still held aloft,
to let the steam rise and open our pores,
to breathe in the buoyant soft air
of invigorating inspiration,
before looking up just in time
to catch the last bus home.

Life Choices

Two Views

This life, huh? Who even knows about it,
but we continue on anyway because
it's mealtime and someone has to cook.
We strive toward ideals
and then have to learn the skills
to accept what actually happens.
Society lauds lofty goals and shiny treasures,
and then we each deal privately
with the real necessities in life—
fortitude, forgiveness, adaptation, love.
Those are the ingredients that make or break a life.
How do we keep going and make a good time of it.
Part of creating a successful, valuable life
involves looking past the highlighted targets
and aiming at those subtle bulls'-eyes
that would create the most difference,
despite what others say,
whether or not anyone else can see them.
I don't understand why there are these two
realities so contrasting—
the public view of life and the private.
But so it is.

O who knows any more [?]

This life, huh? Who even knows about it but we continue on anyway because it's meal time + someone has to cook. We strive toward ideals + then have to learn the skills to actually accept what happens. Society lauds lofty goals + impressive treasures, + then we each deal privately with the real necessities in life — fortitude, forgiveness, adaptation, love. Those are the ingredients that make or break a life. How do we keep going + make a good time of it but by creating a successful balance of life. It involves aiming past the highlighted targets or looking at those subtle bull's-eyes that would create the most difference, despite what others say, whether or not anyone else can see them. I don't understand why there are these two realities so contrary, the public view of life + the private. But so it is

Two Views

55

Sproing

Shaky Lines

Life's a hard story.
Then, it's joyous and full of wonder, deep contentment.
It's meditative and listening to wisdom's diffused voice.
It's a little boring.
It's horrible, unendurable.
It's different than I think it is.
It's changing even now.
Life won't keep
a set
shape.
It doesn't know why I get so worked up.
It's magical,
delighting my secret sense of beauty.
It's the grandest teacher, instructing in its every facet.
It's a letdown, and long.
It's a loop of mundane expectations.
It's a repetition of injuries,
the trapdoor's return,
the soul's chronic wounds.
It's the humbling awareness of other perspectives.
It's the shift that frees the mind,
resurrects the heart.
It's the easy routine of mornings,
the pace of giving effort.
It's the calm oneness of all that is.
It keeps changing
and changing.
And I'm balancing here
like a cartographer trying to map
a wave's rushing crest.

Wake Up!

How do we fall asleep so easily?
Fall asleep right inside our lives,
while still hurdling and racing
through adulthood's challenge course.

Wake up!

For brief spells, we see our own lives,
their million technicolor details
and as-yet unaccepted opportunities.
Why did I never do those things?
we wonder with a pang,
and a whole new life seems within reach—
if we could only cross into the world
suddenly visible around us.

Keep hold of this! we remember
when habitual routines tug at attention.
Remember to breathe
the clearer air of a new moment,
to look at the beauty, at daylight.
Remember that at any second
we can change our eyes, sit up tall,
and be more like ourselves
than we were before.

Some parts of us
are just dreams
it's time to wake from.

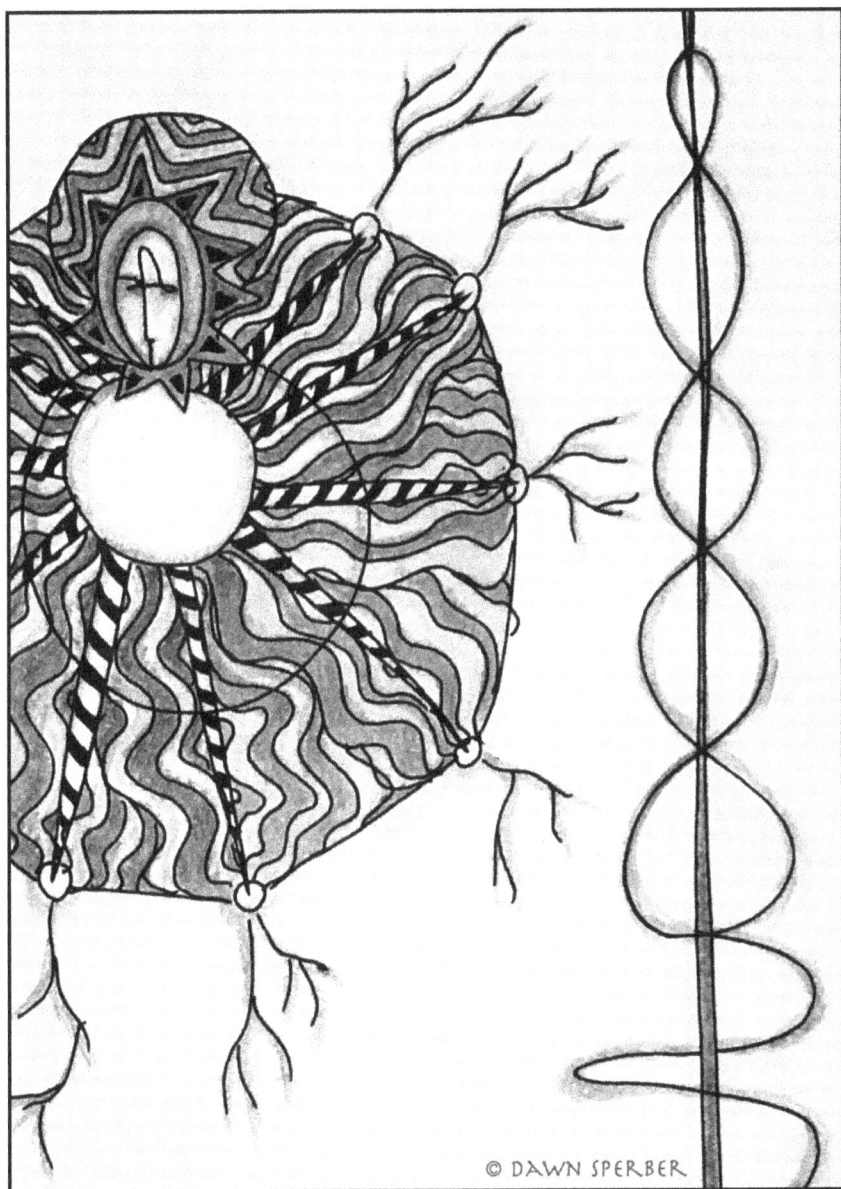

© DAWN SPERBER

Zing

Welcome

Happy birthday to me.
My light's lit, my living's rushing through me.
The ellipses trailing off my stories
are turning on, shining,
floating in spirals around me.

All along I have kept going,
all through my hells I've kept dancing,
and now my cells grow in rhythm
to the beating of my heart.
Even my trips and landings have grace.
I feel like it anyway.
Still here? All this time?
Congratulations, soul in a body,
mind in a soul,
body growing stronger still. Aw yeah.

Another year, another trip past Go.
A little bit more awake this time,
gears greased and ready,
with less to lose and more to rely on,
outside of me and inside, respectively.

I'm coming out of last year
with so many dragon heads
dangling from my grip,
my delicate footsteps dancing
across the burning delusions
like footstones in my path.

As I keep wandering through the world
on my twisty-twirly
labyrinthine journey,
having all sorts of heroic adventures
masked as mundane requirements.

But I know better.
I know I'm alive and this thing's on.
—Check, 1, 2, 3—
Welcome. I'm just winging it as I go.
Let's enjoy the show.

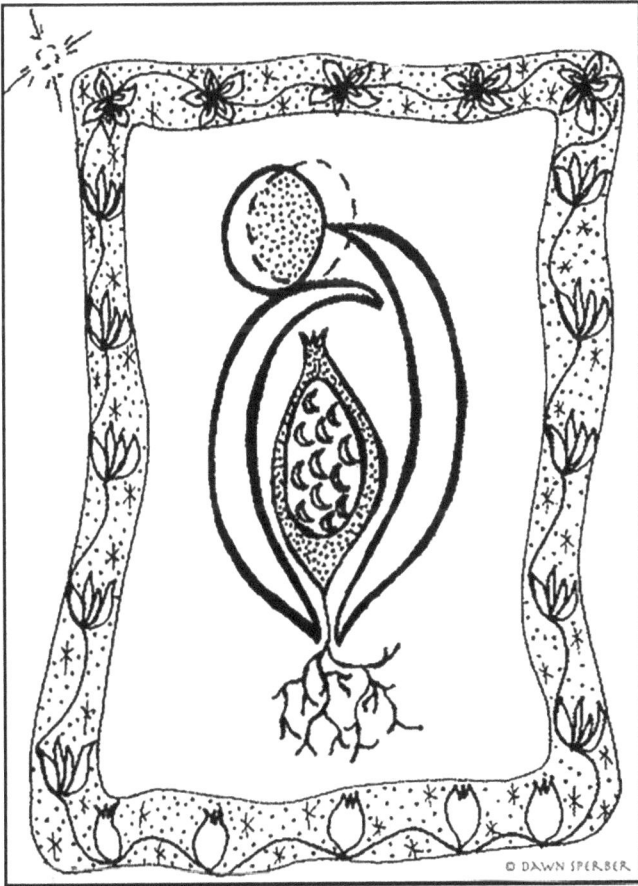

Eclipse

Shadow-dog

I'm trying to record my poems,
and meanwhile, Osito is outside barking away.
Finally, I finish my poem and go outside,
and there's the night all beautiful
and the moon veiled in passing clouds,
and Osito just lays down
in the shadows on the deck
and pretends there's no one barking out there,
not that he knows.
He's just a shadow-dog,
and it's impossible to detect him
if he only moves his eyes.
That's what he tries to convince me.
"Too much barking!" I say.
And he says, Hmm, maybe you're confused.
Only quiet shadows out here.
Maybe you should shut the door
and leave me to these passing moon clouds
and that delicious siren starting up
again a few blocks away
and our deep-voiced neighbor
(Maybe a Doberman?)
"It's too much," I say.
I am a puddle of dark, he says.
"C'mon," I say.
. . . .
(He has to make me wait a beat.)
And then he's a patter of tapping paws,
a skip down the stairs,
and a flip of his long tail
as he turns the corner through the door.
♥ That guy.

Charmed Night

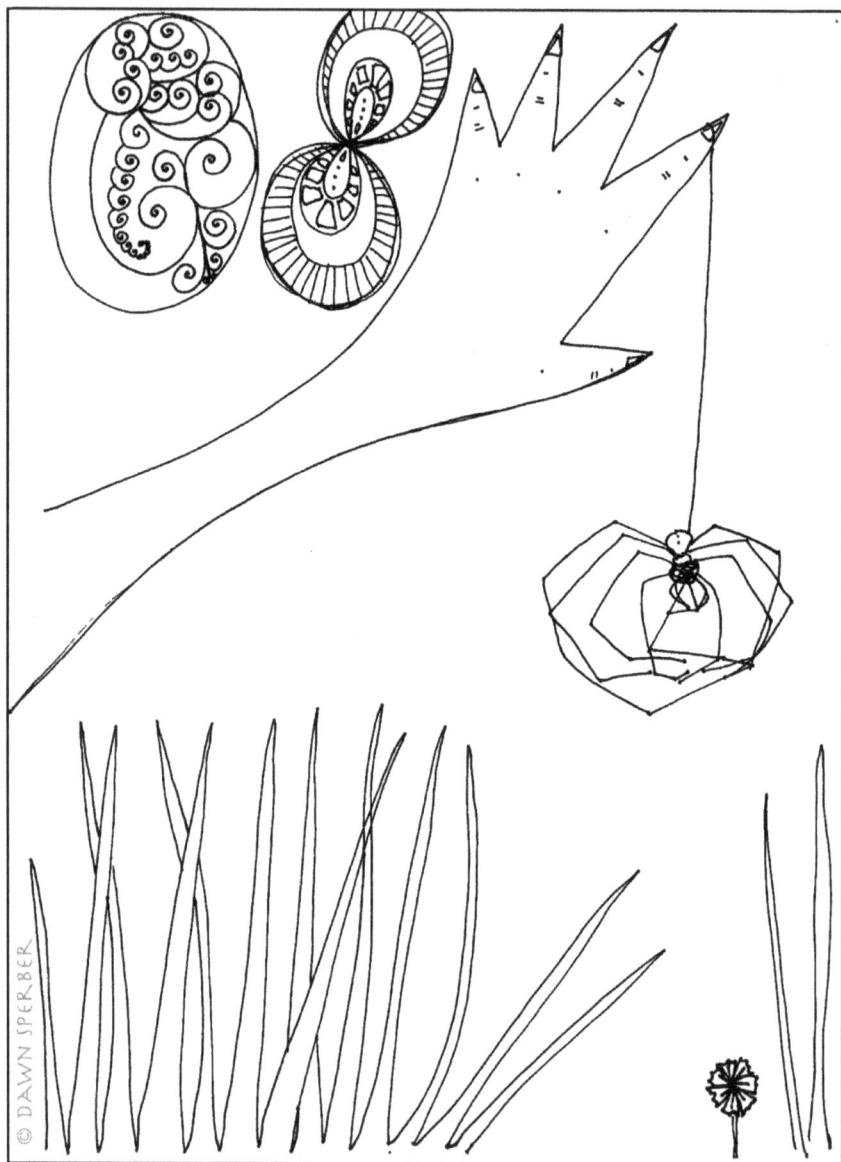

Spider Finger

Spiders Bite Me in My Sleep

Spiders bite me in my sleep,
walking over the great land of me,
all my shifting contours,
and then giving a little nibble
for whatever reason
in certain exact spots.
The back of my hand.
My inside upper arm.
On top of my kneecap.
The small of my back.

Do they suddenly need to test
if the land is made of food?
Am I?
Do they always bite what is beneath them?
Or do they understand that I am sleeping
and walk like kings across my mammoth stillness,
stretching their legs long,
taking their time,
and leaning down to chomp
whenever the whim takes hold.

Maybe they're trying to taste my dreams.
Maybe they do.

I itch from where they've tasted me,
their little bites of ownership.
Red dots like planted flags.
I am a part of their kingdom,
and then the land of me wakes
to walk out far into the world,
spreading word of the spiders' claim.

Working on It

Light in the Night of My Body

I bet there are certain words
waiting in caves inside of me—
you know how I have all these caves,
and some are filled with water
and some are filled with bats
and some are full of words,
little secret and quiet words
that sparkle better than any
stars reflected on the water
(and that's some of the best shine).

My words are treasures,
especially the unmined ones, still
connected to my stone walls.
Some of my words are like geodes
filled with watch parts
and they tick and click gears,
thrumming while they do their light-spill.
Don't you know.

Inside my caves, there are
mothers calling for their children,
leaning out the cave door and throwing
their voices out into the night of my body,
because the mothers who are certain words
can't find their daughters who are also my words,
and like so do the unconscious processes
of my knowing
enact their dramas inside me.

—continued

Inside me, there are the tragedies
of obstacles to understandings,
for so many consciousnesses
and voices live within,
and they're reaching out for each other,
longing to make connections and grow insight
during this carnival ride of my lifetime.

Sometimes, the smallest misalignment of moments
can interrupt that connection of disparate knowledges
that could have bred epiphany. Tragic.
That's why the women call for their babes
between my bones.

But when the voices choir and harmonize,
ringing their sweet shared song throughout my being—
bless this body and all its breathing pores,
bless these hands spilling letters
and sentences from my fingertips,
bless this tongue shaping spoken sounds.
I'm blessed to be the unity of these voices together,
singing into me their realizations and understandings,
as I one by one pluck words, knit thoughts, share insights.
Fulfilling the duty of this lifetime.

I contain a city and how could a city not speak its mind
(mind being that invisible thread stitching togetherness).
Speak up, civilization inside me.
Sing out, dynasties of ancient DNA
that whisper their fragmented hints.
Let's all grab hold of the moment's reigns,
share ideas, remember our origins, and understand.
Each of us contain such worlds.
The answers to all questions
live in our body's caves and shoals.

So much depends on arrangements and timing.
Pluck words, spill truth,
relieve the pressure a little more,
and sway to the clicking
of the clock gears in my geodes.
Like so many hearts.
Like a buzzing hive of realizers.
Body spill, word stream, truth zephyr,
carry us onward.

The Muse Stands on My House

The Woman Who Is This Day

This day is slinking up around me,
intoxicating me with its hundred fingers
flickering around my face and neck,
like the most luxurious woman.
O, the woman who is this day.

I want to wander through her,
and it's hard to think straight,
to keep on track when she keeps doing this,
entrancing me and tickling over my skin.
She makes me want to do not much,
but devote all my attention to her,
to smell her breath, and feel her sighs
press back my shirt sleeves
when I ride my bike through her,
as her fingers stroke my hair
into ribbons that tap my back.

—continued

Every single thing her gaze falls on brightens,
so that the whole day is flirted with
and glows with her charms.
We're all in love
with the same woman who is this day,
and we wear tank tops and skirts for her,
showing those arms and legs
we hid from winter's pinches, and
she kisses our cheeks and noses to blushes,
welcoming us back,
confident and self-possessed
as if she's always been here so bright and warm,
and it is we who went astray
but have found our way back home.

This day gives me ideas, re-ignites old dreams,
of road trips, hot springs, love and adventure,
of being insouciant, and remembering
to stretch out my body,
and that it is beautiful.
O, this day.

I want to lean her over this table
and kiss her long and so soft,
but I don't know where her mouth is,
and maybe her mouth is everywhere,
like her gaze is, and her beautiful fingers.
If this day were a mortal
who loved me with such brilliance,
I'd extend my ring finger with an "Always."
As it is, with her,
this Empress all-loving goddess,
I breathe her in and I breathe her out,
smile, and say her name.
"Today."

Petal Booklet

Imagine
if I gave you a booklet
made of flower petals. Just because.
A very small book, a petal per a page,
fresh, instantly made, no time to wilt.
And maybe you'd be given a fly's eyes
with which to read the moist book,
so you could clearly see the fragile veins
written within the pages like sonnets,
and the glittery shimmer the petals cast in sunlight.
You'd hold the book on the fingerprint of one finger
and turn the pages with a blade of grass.
And after you read the book with your eyes,
you could then read it with your nose.
Open it up and lay the pages on your nostrils,
inhale the fluttering fragrance of the tale
and know it beyond words or vision.
This   small   book,   know   it,
absorb it with every sense quickly;
then before it wrinkles in the air,
lay it on your tongue
and swallow.

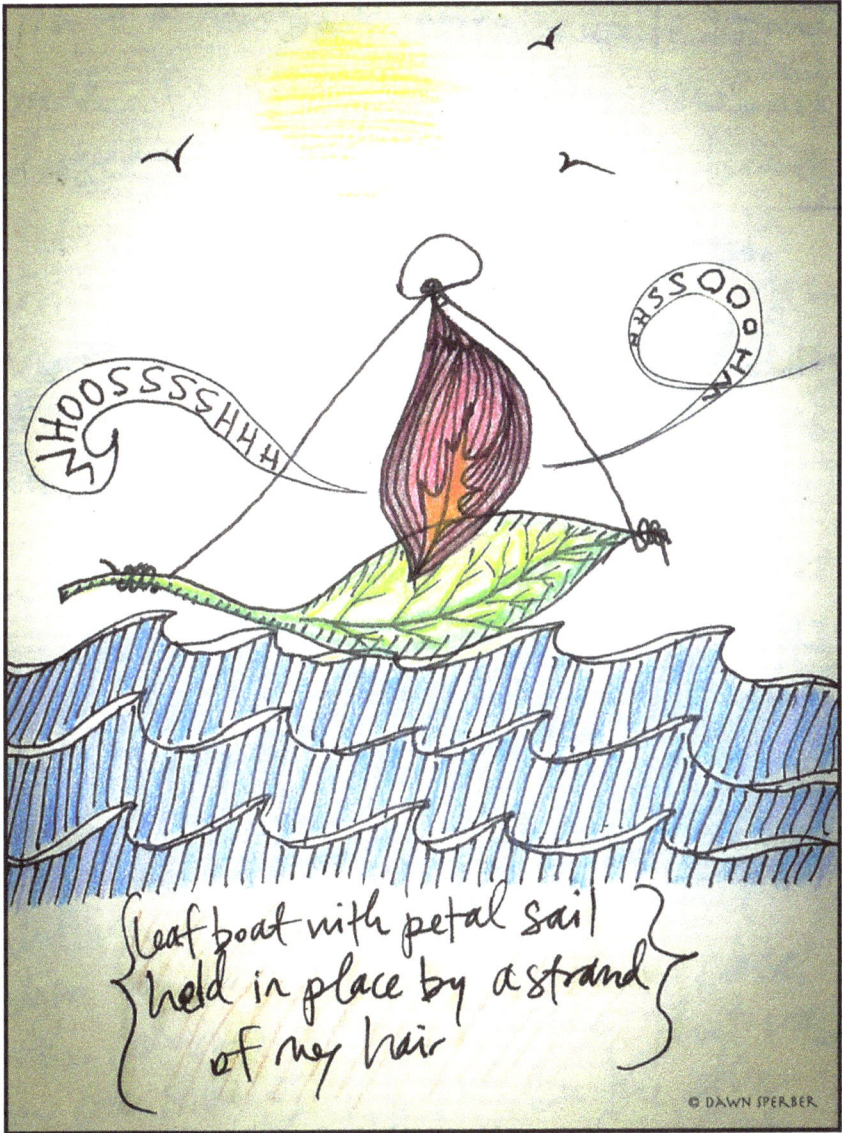

Leaf Boat

Gentle, Gentle, Go My Friend

Gentle, gentle, go my friend.
Step over mysterious stones.
Don't bother to give them tread,
but leave them each alone.

Look how your feet are like little sighs
or creek glistens in the light,
and deserve the moss and green,
the steps the loving earth receives—

But not the tumbling (gasp!) surprise,
when foot on unsure rock collide.
And tumble, Roar, turn wide the ground—
reveals the dragon's sleeping mound!

His eyes peek wide,
when they blink, go hide!
This is where the faeries run
and slip up, wink out, like sparks of sun.

Gentle, gentle, go my friend.
Step over mysterious stones.
Don't deign to give them tread,
but do dance on, and delight your home!

Harpy Dragon

A Small Love, Obviously Wild

It was a small love I found in my pocket one day,
while I walked a mountain trail
leading to a wildflower-lit meadow.
Loves can come in all shapes and sizes.
This was a love for the wild day,
which smelled like mint and sweet grass,
pine trees and coyote scat and ozone clean.
It was a day when I felt ancient and timeless
like I'd been walking forest paths for centuries,
my pulse matched to my gait, while my head
flickered through ideas and dreams.
I mean, my moment fit me so securely.
And that's when I reached into my shirt pocket
and found the small love.

The love's heartbeat quick as a tickling fingertip.
It was leopard-spotted, obviously wild, the size of a shrew,
with the wings that all loves wear.
Softly, it hummed a song I almost remembered.
When I looked at it too long and closely,
it thrummed its wings, lifted its slight weight
from my palm, and flew over to a stand of columbines.
I was a little hurt, till I saw it was clutching
one of my shirt collar buttons in its wee paws
like a love token. To me, the small theft
tasted sweet as the drop from a honeysuckle's stamen.
My love for that day still lives
among those mountain columbines,
though these days,
it carries my button in its cheek.

© DAWN SPERBER

Little Love

Soul Warrior

Come to Me, Goodness

Come to me, goodness.
GOODNESS! GRACE!
The moving forward on the good path's ground.
Come to me now.

Look at these cuddly years passing,
scampering their wee bodies over this big plush couch.
Innocuous, till—Shoot, where'd they go?
All those little years, running around underfoot.
I'll just keep calling for the life I want.
GOODNESS! GRACE!

Come find me on the battlefield.
Offer me your hand, and I'll rise like a kite.
We'll stride through the fighting
and leave a tinkling armory landing on the tilled ground.
Without weapons, opponents will be revealed as neighbors
and walk on to care for their daily needs.
Life will proceed.
Anger will evaporate like puddles,
and then the rain will fall, and the sun will shine,
and this field will bloom with irises
like forgiveness and resurrection. So mote it be.
GOODNESS! Come, come, come.
GRACE! Please enter.

May my force be a mirror
that helps Light travel
to where it needs to go.

Please help this life to shine.

What Are We Waiting For?

I bet there are forests who miss me,
who wish I were a squirrel in their trees
or a supposedly mythical mermaid in their ponds.
I bet there are kisses who wish I were in them too,
because they like my technique.
I bet there are sunrays looking for me even now,
not yet knowing I've gone indoors.
There may also be songs wishing I'd turn them on,
and others who wish I was already dancing to them.
I wonder if there are dresses that wish I were wearing them
instead of someone else or getting left on the hanger.
I bet there are houses that wish I were living in them,
maybe houses that I'll one day move in and dance through,
but not yet; I haven't yet even visited their towns,
and the houses shift and groan their tree trunks and wonder,
Why do I have to wait?
Because they want me, see. Because it'll be that good.

And so I ask my future and all my possibilities
and all my impossible, perfect, fantastical dreams
to call for me LOUD, light road flares,
use spotlights, catch me with a stage hook
and reel me in close.
Because, if I want you and you want me,
I tell my future, what are we waiting for?
It's only ellipses dividing us.
Let us blow them away like breadcrumbs . . .

I love to long for my future,
and I love when my future longs for me.
It feels as good as dancing to the most kickass song,
when my body predicts beats and breaks
and rhythm changes, when it's all tight and suave,
like all I've been waiting for is right here,
and I'm drinkin' it down easy.
And really, when life's like that,

when I'm drunk on dreams and slippery with time,
nothing can hold me back, not rules or logic,
and beauty breaks all boundaries.
I burst through the seams, racing my bike
down the streets, free in the world:
this wildly improbable.

Birdgirl

Sometimes life takes center stage, & my writing sits politely to the side, with its hands (all its many hands) in its lap, waiting for its turn. I say, come on, join in, let's all be together. But the writing seems to like it me & her, with our breaths mixing as we lean in close to each other, telling secrets that've never before seen the light of day. She smiles & shakes her head, waits for me to come to her with the right mood wrapped around me.

© DAWN SPERBER

Writing Sits Politely

Dawn Sperber is the author of *Now, That's a Trick* (Finishing Line Press, 2022), a magical realism chapbook of flash fiction based in New Mexico. Her lyrical stories and poems have appeared in *Daily Science Fiction, PANK Magazine, Bourbon Penn, NANO Fiction, Hunger Mountain, Gargoyle, Zizzle Literary, Luna Station Quarterly, ONE ART, flashquake, Annalemma, The Doctor T.J. Eckleburg Review, Third Wednesday, Witches & Pagans, Rosebud, The Pedestal,* and elsewhere. A writer, editor, and artist in New Mexico and Texas, Dawn is drawn to authenticity, healing, and pursuing the mojo that motors us through the challenges. Find her at dawnsperber.com.

SHANTI ARTS

NATURE • ART • SPIRIT

Please visit us online
to browse our entire book catalog,
including poetry collections and fiction,
books on travel, nature, healing, art,
photography, and more.

Also take a look at our highly regarded art
and literary journal, *Still Point Arts Quarterly*,
which may be downloaded for free.

www.shantiarts.com

www.ingramcontent.com/pod-product-compliance
Lightning Source LLC
Chambersburg PA
CBHW051214090426
42742CB00022B/3454